D0987642

Punjabi
Subzis

TARLA DALAL
India's #1 Cookery Author

S&C

SANJAY & CO.

MUMBAI

Third Printing : 2008

ISBN 10 : 81-89491-17-2
ISBN 13 : 978-8-189491-17-8

Price: Rs. 89/-

Published & Distributed by : **Sanjay & Company**
353/A-1, Shah & Nahar Industrial Estate, Dhanraj Mill Compound, Lower Parel (W), Mumbai - 400 013. INDIA.
Tel. : (91-22) 2496 8068 • Fax : (91-22) 2496 5876 • E-mail : sanjay@tarladalal.com

---

UK and USA customers can call us on :
UK : 02080029533   ●   USA : 213-634-1406
For books, Membership on **tarladalal.com**, Subscription for **Cooking & More** and Recipe queries
Timing : 9.30 a.m. to 7.00 p.m. (IST), from Monday to Saturday
Local call charges applicable

Recipe Research & Production Design	Nutritionist	Photography	Designed by	Copy Editor
Arati Fedane Umaima Abdulaly	Nisha Katira Sapna Kamdar	Jignesh Jhaveri	Satyamangal Rege	Janani Gopalakrishnan
	Food Styling Shubhangi Dhaimade	**Typesetting** Adityas Enterprises	**Printed by :** Minal Sales Agencies, Mumbai	

BULK PURCHASES : Tarla Dalal Cookbooks are ideal gifts. If you are interested in buying more than 500 assorted copies of Tarla Dalal Cookbooks at special prices, please contact us at 91-22-2496 8068 or email : sanjay@tarladalal.com

INTRODUCTION

Dear friends,

A lot of people in India and abroad identify Indian cuisine with Punjabi food. For them, Indian food is almost synonymous with *naans*, gravied vegetables, curries and *pulaos*.

For the many cooking enthusiasts eager to experiment with authentic Punjabi cuisine, this book serves as a window into the region's versatile *subzis*.

Punjab! The very name reminds one of rich and creamy gravies, laden with bountiful vegetables and aromatic spices. Punjabi gravies make abundant use of ghee and cream, and the basic *masala* in most Punjabi dishes consists of onion, ginger, *kasuri methi* and a lot of tomatoes fried in pure ghee. Though I have modified many of the recipes by substituting oil for ghee, those of you who are not overly health conscious can feel free to perk up your gravies with butter, ghee and cream!

Though Punjabi cuisine is quite popular for its non-vegetarian dishes, the vegetarian dishes and adapted versions of non-vegetarian dishes are equally enticing.

This book includes not only world famous recipes but also lesser-known ones, which I have collected, especially for you, from many of my Punjabi friends. In addition to popular dishes like **Malai Kofta, Khoya Mutter Makhana, Rajma** and **Sarson ka Saag** and a whole section dedicated to Paneer recipes, this book also includes lip smacking recipes using seasonal ingredients like **Shalgam** and **Kamal Kakdi**.

Delight by taking your pick from this *khazana* of authentic, tasty, and easy to follow Punjabi recipes. In cooking, the journey is as pleasurable as the destination. So, enjoy every minute of it!

Regards,

Tarla Dalal

CONTENTS

❦ Achaari Dahi Bhindi ❦

Picture on page 2.

With pungent achaari spices and tangy curds, bhindi takes a new aavtar.

Preparation time: 10 minutes.   Cooking time: 25 minutes.   Serves 4.

500 gms (approx 30 nos) ladies finger *(bhindi)*
2 tsp chopped ginger
¾ cup chopped tomatoes
¼ cup fresh thick curds *(dahi)*
¼ tsp turmeric powder *(haldi)*
¾ tsp chilli powder
2 tsp coriander *(dhania)* powder
4 tbsp oil
Salt to taste

For the achaari masala
2 tsp fennel seeds *(saunf)*
1 tsp mustard seeds *(rai / sarson)*
½ tsp onion seeds *(kalongi)*
¼ tsp fenugreek *(methi)* seeds
A pinch of asafoetida *(hing)*

1. Wash, wipe dry and slit the ladies finger into half and then cut them into 25 mm. (1 ") pieces.
2. Heat 2 tbsp of oil in a pan and sauté the ladies finger in it , in 2 batches. Keep aside.
3. Heat 2 tbsp of oil another pan and add the achaari masala to it.
4. When the seeds crackle, add the ginger and tomatoes. Sauté for 5 minutes till the mixture leaves oil.
5. Meanwhile whisk together the curds, turmeric powder, chilli powder, coriander powder and salt.
6. Add this mixture to the pan, mix well and cook for a couple of minutes.
7. Add the ladies finger and simmer for 2 minutes.
   Serve hot.

❖ Gobi Simla Mirch ❖

The common cauliflower tastes unbelievably exotic in this spicy curd-based gravy.
As always, capsicum adds a special touch.

Preparation time: 10 minutes. Cooking time: 20 minutes. Serves 4.

2 ½ cups cauliflower, cut into medium sized florets
1 cup capsicum, cut into big cubes
A pinch of turmeric powder (*haldi*)
1 tsp cumin seeds (*jeera*)
½ cup finely chopped onions
½ tbsp ginger-garlic paste
1 tsp chopped green chillies
½ tsp Punjabi *garam masala*, page 100
½ tsp chilli powder
1 tbsp roasted and crushed dried fenugreek leaves (*kasuri methi*)
½ cup tomatoes, cut into large chunks
4 tbsp oil
Salt to taste

For the garnish
2 tbsp chopped coriander

1. Add the turmeric and salt to a vesselful of water and mix well.
2. Soak the cauliflower in it for about 10 minutes. Drain and keep aside.
3. Heat 2 tbsp of oil in a pan and fry the cauliflower in it till it is golden brown.
4. Add the capsicum and sauté for a few more minutes.
5. Heat the remaining oil in a *kadhai* and add the cumin seeds to it.
6. When they crackle, add the onions and sauté till they turn translucent.
7. Add the ginger-garlic paste, green chillies, salt, *Punjabi garam masala*, chilli powder and dried fenugreek leaves and sauté for about a minute.
8. Mix well and add the tomatoes. Sauté for a few minutes and add the cauliflower and capsicum and cook for a while till the vegetables are coated with the masala. Serve hot garnished with coriander.

❖ Subz Do Pyaza ❖

*In this popular gravy, onions are added twice. Not only do they form the base,
but also make their crunchy presence felt amidst the other vegetables!*

Preparation time: 15 minutes.   Cooking time: 20 minutes.   Serves 4.

2 cups mixed boiled vegetables (cauliflower, corn, peas, french beans)
½ cup onion cubes
½ tsp turmeric powder *(haldi)*
½ tsp chilli powder
1 tsp coriander *(dhania)* powder
¾ cup fresh tomato purée, page 102
1 tsp Punjabi *garam masala,* page 100
2 tbsp fresh cream
4 tbsp oil
Salt to taste

To be ground into a paste
1 cup chopped onions

3 cloves garlic

For the garnish
2 tbsp chopped coriander

1. Heat 1 tbsp of oil in a pan and sauté the onion cubes in it till they are translucent. Remove and keep aside.
2. Add the remaining oil to the same pan and fry the prepared paste in it till it turns golden brown.
3. Add the turmeric powder, chilli powder, coriander powder and salt. Sprinkle 2 tbsp water and fry the masala mixture for a few more minutes.
4. Add tomato purée and cook till the mixture leaves oil.
5. Add the vegetables, sautéed onions and ½ cup of water. Mix well and cover the pan with lid and cook till onions are soft.
6. Remove the lid, mix in the Punjabi *garam masala* and serve hot garnished with coriander.

❧ Khatte Aloo ❧

Combining the khatta flavour of dry mango powder with the distinct tastes of other spices, this potato subzi throws a challenge to the diners no one can stop with just one helping.

Preparation time: 10 minutes.   Cooking time: 25 minutes.   Serves 4.

4 cups whole baby potatoes, washed and peeled
1 tsp carom seeds *(ajwain)*
2 tsp dry mango powder *(amchur)*
1 tsp Punjabi *garam masala,* page 100
1 tbsp coriander *(dhania)* powder
1 tbsp cumin seed *(jeera)* powder
¾ cup cherry tomatoes
1 cup fresh thick curds *(dahi)*, whisked
3 tbsp oil
Salt to taste

1. Parboil the potatoes in a vesselful of salted water. Drain and keep aside.

2. Heat the oil in a *kadhai*, add the carom seeds and potatoes.
3. Sauté well till the potatoes are crisp.
4. Add the dry mango powder, Punjabi *garam* masala, coriander powder and cumin seed powder and sauté for a few more minutes.
5. Add the cherry tomatoes and 2 tbsp of water and heat till the potatoes are completely cooked and crisp to taste.
6. Add the curds and ½ cup of water and bring to a boil.
   Serve hot.

Handy tip : Choose small potatoes that are equal in size for this recipe.

❖ Baigan Bhurta ❖

Roasted brinjals cooked in tangy tomato gravy, this is one brinjal preparation that no one can say no to. The success of this recipe lies in how well you roast the brinjals.

Preparation time: 15 minutes.   Cooking time: 15 minutes.   Serves 4.

2 big brinjals *(baingan)*
1½ cups sliced onions
12 mm. (½") piece ginger, peeled and cut into thin strips
2 green chillies, thinly sliced
1 tsp chilli powder
1½ cups tomato slices
¼ cup chopped coriander
2 tbsp ghee
Salt to taste

1. Wash and dry the brinjals. Apply little oil on them and roast on low flame till they soften and turn black.
2. Cool the brinjals, peel the skin and mash them.

3. Heat the ghee in a pan and add the onions, ginger and green chillies and sauté them till the onions turn translucent.
4. Add the chilli powder, tomatoes, mashed brinjals and cook till the ghee separates from the gravy.
5. Add the coriander and mix well.
   Serve hot.

❖ Rajma ❖

Picture on facing page.

A world famous recipe from the kitchens of Punjab, this makes for a delicious and wholesome meal when served with chawal.

Preparation time: 10 minutes.   Cooking time: 15 minutes.   Serves 4.

¾ cup kashmiri *rajma* (red kidney beans), soaked overnight
½ tsp cumin seeds *(jeera)*
25 mm. (1") stick cinnamon *(dalchini)*
½ cup sliced onions
1 tbsp thinly sliced ginger
2 slit green chillies
¼ tsp turmeric powder *(haldi)*
2 tbsp coriander *(dhania)* powder
1½ tbsp dry mango powder *(amchur)*
½ tsp black salt *(sanchal)*
2 tbsp oil
Salt to taste

RAJMA : Recipe above. ➜

For the garnish
2 tbsp chopped coriander

1. Drain the water from the *rajma*, wash and keep aside.
2. Heat the oil in a pressure cooker and add cumin seeds and cinnamon.
3. When they crackle, add the onions and sauté for a few minutes till they turn translucent.
4. Add the ginger and green chillies and sauté for a few more minutes.
5. Add the soaked rajma, alongwith 3 cups of water, turmeric powder, coriander powder and salt. Pressure cook for 4 to 5 whistles.
6. When the pressure is released, add the dry mango powder and black salt, mix well and simmer for a few more minutes.
   Serve hot garnished with coriander.

Handy tip: Kashmiri *rajma* is the smaller, darker coloured variety of *rajma*.

❀ Subz Bhurji ❀

A bhurji is a preparation which involves mashing all the ingredients together well.

Preparation time: 10 minutes.   Cooking time: 10 minutes.   Serves 4.

½ cup boiled potatoes, cut into cubes
½ cup *paneer* (cottage cheese), cut into big pieces
½ cup boiled green peas
½ cup sliced mushrooms
2 tsp *chaat masala*
2 tsp roasted dried fenugreek powder *(kasuri methi)*
½ cup chopped onions
½ tsp chilli powder
½ tsp chopped green chillies
¼ tsp turmeric powder *(haldi)*
1 tbsp chopped coriander
3 tbsp oil
Salt to taste

For the garnish
2 tbsp chopped coriander

1. Mix the potatoes, *paneer*, peas, mushrooms, *chaat masala*, dried fenugreek leaves and salt. Keep aside.
2. Heat the oil on a large *tava*, add the onions and sauté till they turn translucent.
3. Add the chilli powder, green chillies, turmeric powder and salt and sauté for a few seconds.
4. Add the vegetable mixture and coriander and cook for some time mashing continuously till the mixture dries up.
   Serve hot garnished with coriander.

❖ Pindi Chole ❖

Picture on page 1.

A popular variation of the versatile chole, this is different from the regular preparation in terms of texture and colour. Pindi chole is a dry dish, where the chole are coated very lightly with the gravy. Tea leaves give this dish its rich colour.

Preparation time: 15 minutes.   Cooking time: 25 minutes.   Serves 4.

1 cup *kabuli chana* (chick peas), soaked overnight
2 tbsp *chana dal* (Bengal gram dal), soaked overnight
2 big cardamom (elaichi)
25 mm. (1") stick cinnamon (dalchini)
¼ tsp soda-bi-carb
2 tsp tea leaves
½ cup grated onion
1½ tsp pomegranate seed (*anardana*) powder
1 tsp ginger paste
1 tsp thinly sliced green chillies
1 tsp coriander *(dhania)* powder
1 tsp Punjabi *garam masala*, page 100

½ tsp chilli powder
¾ cup fresh tomato purée, page 102
2 tsp chole masala
4 tbsp oil
Salt to taste

For the garnish
2 tbsp grated paneer (optional)

1. Drain and wash the *kabuli chana* and *chana dal*. Keep aside.
2. Make a small *potli* by tying the cardamom, cinnamon and tea leaves in a 2" x 2" piece of muslin cloth.
3. Pressure cook the *kabuli chana*, *chana dal*, the *potli*, soda-bi-carb, salt and 2½ cups of water for 2 whistles.
4. Discard the potli and keep aside.
5. Heat the oil in a *kadhai*, add the onions and sauté till they are golden brown.
6. Add in the pomegranate seed powder, ginger paste, green chillies, coriander powder, Punjabi *garam masala* and chilli powder.
7. Add the tomato purée and salt and cook till the oil separates from the gravy.
8. Add the *kabuli chana* and *chana dal* alongwith the water and *chole masala*.
9. Cook till the *chole* is completely dry.
   Serve hot garnished with paneer.

❖ Aloo Methi ❖

This winning combination of potatoes and fresh fenugreek leaves, in a dry curry form, is very common in every north Indian home.

Preparation time: 15 minutes.   Cooking time: 15 minutes.   Serves 4.

1½ cups peeled and boiled potatoes
4 cups fresh fenugreek *(methi)* leaves
1 tsp cumin seeds *(jeera)*
1 tsp chopped garlic
1 tbsp chopped ginger
2 whole dry red chillies, dry roasted and broken into pieces
1 tsp finely chopped green chillies
2 tsp coriander *(dhania)* powder
½ tsp turmeric powder *(haldi)*
¼ tsp asafoetida *(hing)*
4 tbsp oil
Salt to taste

1. Wash the fenugreek leaves and chop them finely. Sprinkle some salt over them and keep aside for about half an hour.
2. Squeeze out all the water and keep aside.
3. Heat the oil in a pan and add the cumin seeds.
4. When they crackle, add the garlic, ginger, red chillies and salt.
5. Add the potatoes and stir-fry for about 5 minutes.
6. Add the fenugreek leaves, coriander powder, turmeric powder and asafoetida.
   Cook covered for 10 minutes on a low flame.
   Serve hot.

Variation : GOBHI METHI : Use 1½ cups of boiled cauliflower instead of potatoes in the above recipe.

SHALGAM METHI : Use 1½ cups of boiled turnips instead of potatoes in the above recipe.

❖ Masala Masoor ❖

Lentils are an indispensable part of Punjabi cuisine. This spicy masoor dal preparation will not fail to tingle your taste buds.

Preparation time: 10 minutes.   Cooking time: 40 minutes.   Serves 4.

¾ cup whole *masoor dal* (whole red lentils), soaked
7 to 8 small white onions, peeled
½ cup sliced onions
½ cup chopped tomatoes
4 tbsp oil
Salt to taste

To be ground into a paste
4 cloves garlic
4 whole dry red chillies, broken into pieces
2 tsp coriander *(dhania)* seeds
1 tsp cumin seeds *(jeera)*
25 mm. (1") piece ginger

¼ cup water

For the garnish
2 tbsp chopped coriander

1. Wash the *masoor dal*, add 1 cup of water, the white onions and salt and cook in a
   pressure cooker for about 1 whistle.
2. Heat the oil in a large pan. Add the sliced onions to it and sauté till they turn
   translucent.
3. Add the ground paste and cook for 4 to 5 minutes.
4. Add the tomatoes and salt and cook while stirring continuously till the mixture
   leaves oil and mix well.
5. Add the cooked *masoor dal* and simmer for 3 to 4 minutes.
   Serve hot garnished with coriander.

❖ Mutter Tamatar ❖

Kasuri methi adds a delicate flavour to this simple combination of peas and tomatoes simmered in curd-based gravy.

Preparation time: 10 minutes.   Cooking time: 20 minutes.   Serves 4.

1½ cup boiled green peas
1½ cups tomatoes, cut into 8 pieces
4 tbsp cashewnuts *(kaju)*, soaked in ¼ cup water
¾ cup fresh thick curds *(dahi)*
1 tsp cardamom *(elaichi)*
½ tsp cumin seeds *(jeera)*
2 tsp dried fenugreek leaves *(kasuri methi)*
1 tsp coriander *(dhania)* powder
½ tsp Punjabi *garam masala*, page 100
½ cup milk
Salt to taste

To be ground into onion-ginger paste
2 medium sized onions
12 mm. (½ ") piece ginger

For the garnish
2 tbsp chopped coriander

1. Drain the cashewnuts, add the cashewnuts, curds and cardamom and blend them together to make a smooth paste.
2. Heat the oil in a pan and add the cumin seeds. When they crackle, add the onion-ginger paste and sauté till it is golden brown.
3. Add the dried fenugreek leaves, coriander powder, Punjabi *garam masala,* salt and the prepared cashewnut paste. Cook till the oil separates from the gravy.
4. Add the milk and ½ cup of water. Simmer till the gravy thickens.
5. Add the peas and tomatoes and cook for 2 minutes.
   Serve hot garnished with coriander.

❧ Aloo Gobhi ❧

A regular in a Punjabi household can be eaten with puris for breakfast or as an evening snack.

Preparation time: 15 minutes.   Cooking time: 20 minutes.   Serves 4.

1½ cups boiled potatoes, peeled and cut into large cubes
1½ cups cauliflower, cut into big florets
1 tsp cumin seeds *(jeera)*
4 whole dry red chillies, broken into pieces
1 tbsp chopped ginger
1 tsp chopped garlic
1 tsp chopped green chillies
½ cup chopped tomatoes
¼ tsp turmeric powder *(haldi)*
1 tsp chilli powder
½ tsp Punjabi *garam masala,* page 100
A pinch asafoetida *(hing)*
1 tbsp lemon juice

2 tbsp chopped coriander
4 tbsp oil
Salt to taste

1. Heat the oil in a pan and add the cumin seeds. When they crackle, add the dry red chillies, ginger, garlic and green chillies.
2. Add the cauliflower and salt. Mix well and cook for a few minutes till the cauliflower florets get a slight brown colour.
3. Add the tomatoes, turmeric powder, chilli powder, Punjabi *garam masala*, asafoetida and 1 cup of water. Cook for 10 minutes till the vegetables are tender.
4. Add the potatoes, lemon juice and coriander.
5. Mix well and cook till all the water dries up.
   Serve hot.

❦ Papite ke Kofte ❧

These raw papaya koftas are authentically Punjabi and not too well-known outside of the state. Try this recipe, straight from the kitchens of Punjab...

Preparation time: 15 minutes.   Cooking time: 20 minutes.   Serves 4.

For the koftas
1½ cups grated raw papaya (*papita*)
1 cup boiled and mashed potatoes
1 tsp dry mango powder (*amchur*)
½ tsp turmeric powder (*haldi*)
1 tsp chilli powder
1 tsp Punjabi *garam masala,* page 100
Oil for deep-frying
Salt to taste

For the gravy
1 cup chopped onions
2 tbsp broken cashewnuts (*kaju*)

½ tsp cumin seeds (*jeera*)
½ tsp chopped garlic
½ tsp chopped ginger
1 tsp thinly sliced green chillies
½ tsp coriander (*dhania*) powder
½ tsp chilli powder
¼ tsp turmeric powder (*haldi*)
1½ cups chopped tomatoes
¼ tsp Punjabi *garam masala,* page 100
2 tbsp cream
3 tbsp oil
Salt to taste

For the garnish
2 tbsp chopped coriander

For the koftas
1. Squeeze the grated papaya till all the water drains out.
2. Add the remaining ingredients, mix well and divide into 8 equal sized koftas.
3. Heat the oil in a pan and deep-fry the koftas till golden brown.
4. Drain on absorbent paper and keep aside.

For the gravy

1. Heat 1 tbsp of the oil in pan, add the cashewnuts and sauté till they turn golden brown.
2. Remove the cashewnuts, drain out the oil and blend them to a smooth paste. Keep aside.
3. Heat the remaining oil in the same pan and add the cumin seeds.
4. When they crackle, add the onions and sauté till they turn translucent.
5. Add the garlic, ginger and green chillies ad sauté for another minute.
6. Add the coriander powder, chilli powder, turmeric powder and tomatoes.
7. Cook till the oil separates from the gravy.
8. Add the prepared browned cashewnut paste, Punjabi *garam masala,* cream and salt and bring to a boil.

How to proceed

Add the *koftas* to the gravy and simmer for a few minutes.
Serve hot garnished with coriander.

Variation: GHIA KOFTA CURRY

Use the *ghia* (white pumkin / *doodhi* / *lauki*) instead of raw papaya to make the koftas. After grating the ghia make sure to squeeze out its water before use.

⟨ Vegetable Hariyali ⟩

Picture on facing page.

*Mixed vegetables cooked in a rare blend of spinach pulp with luscious white gravy.
The white gravy can be made a week before and used for a number of dishes. Do not
over cook the gravy as far as possible to maintain the colour of the dish.*

Preparation time: 15 minutes.   Cooking time: 15 minutes.   Serves 4.

1 cup mixed boiled vegetables (carrots, French beans, cauliflower, green peas, baby
corn etc.)
¼ cup cherry tomatoes (optional)
¼ cup chopped capsicum
1 tsp ginger-garlic paste
½ cup white gravy, recipe below
1 tbsp tomato purée, page 102
1 tbsp cream
1 tsp lemon juice
¼ tsp Punjabi *garam masala,* page 100
1 tbsp butter
Salt to taste

VEGETABLE HARIYALI : Recipe above. ↪

36

To be ground into a hariyali paste
1 cup blanched and chopped spinach *(palak)*
¼ cup chopped mint leaves (phudina)
A pinch of turmeric powder *(haldi)*
1 green chilli

For the white gravy
½ cup sliced onions
5 cashewnuts *(kaju)*
1 tbsp melon seeds *(charmagaz)*
2 green chillies

For the white gravy
1. Combine all the ingredients with ¾ cup of water and simmer for about 15 minutes.
2. Cool and blend to a smooth paste. Keep aside.

How to proceed
1. Heat the butter in a pan, add the capsicum and sauté for 2 to 3 minutes.
2. Add the ginger-garlic paste and sauté for 1 more minute.
3. Add the white gravy, tomato purée and ½ cup water and allow it to simmer for 2 to 3 minutes.
4. Add the hariyali paste, cream and salt and mix well.
5. Allow it to simmer for 3 to 5 minutes, then add the lemon juice, salt, Punjabi *garam masala,* boiled vegetables and cherry tomatoes and mix well.
6. Simmer for a couple of more minutes.
   Serve hot.

❖ Aloo Mutter Tariwale ❖

Aloo and peas cooked in rich curd-based gravy. Although it may take longer, it is good to cook the vegetables in the gravy itself as it absorbs the flavour well.

Preparation time: 15 minutes.   Cooking time: 25 minutes.   Serves 4.

1½ cups boiled and cubed potatoes
1½ cups boiled green peas
2 green cardamom *(elaichi)*
1 bayleaf *(tejpatta)*
2 tsp ginger-garlic paste
½ cup fresh thick curds, whisked
¼ tsp turmeric powder *(haldi)*
¼ tsp chilli powder
¼ tsp Punjabi *garam masala,* page 100
½ tsp sugar
2 tbsp fresh cream
3 tsp oil
Salt to taste

For the white gravy
½ cup sliced onions
3 tbsp cashewnuts (*kaju*)
1 to 2 tbsp melon seeds (*charmagaz*)
2 green chillies

For the garnish
2 tbsp chopped coriander

For the white gravy
1. Add all the ingredients to ¾ cup of water and cook on a slow flame for about 15 minutes.
2. Cool and blend to a smooth paste. Keep aside.

How to proceed
1. Heat the oil in a pan, add the cardamom, bayleaf and ginger-garlic paste and sauté for a few seconds.
2. Add the curds, turmeric powder, chilli powder and the white gravy.
3. Mix well and cook for 2 to 3 minutes stirring continuously so the gravy does not curdle.
4. Add the potatoes, peas, Punjabi *garam masala*, sugar, cream, salt and ½ cup of water and simmer for about 5 minutes.
   Serve hot garnished with coriander.

Paneer Khaas

◈ Palak Paneer ◈

Palak or saag is one of the favourite leafy vegetables in north Indian households.
They use the versatile palak in a variety of preparations such as raita,
gravy and even kofta!

Preparation time: 15 minutes.   Cooking time: 25 minutes.   Serves 2.

2 cups *paneer* (cottage cheese) cubes
6 cups washed and chopped spinach (*palak*) leaves
1 tsp garlic paste
1 tsp ginger paste
1 tsp dried fenugreek leaves (*kasuri methi*)
1 tsp Punjabi *garam masala,* page 100
1 tsp sugar
¼ cup cream
¼ cup finely chopped tomatoes

41

¼ tsp black salt
2 tsp oil
1 tsp butter
Salt to taste

For the white gravy
1 cup sliced onions
3 tbsp cashewnuts (*kaju*)
1 tbsp melon seeds (*charmagaz*)
2 green chillies

For the white gravy
1. Combine all the ingredients with 1 cup of water and simmer for about 15 minutes.
2. Cool and blend to a smooth paste. Keep aside.

How to proceed
1. Boil 4 cups of water with salt and cook the spinach leaves in it till tender. Take care not to loose colour of the leaves.
2. Remove from flame and drain. Blend to a smooth purée.
3. Heat the oil and butter in a pan and add the ginger, garlic and tomatoes to it.
4. Sauté for sometime till the mixture leaves oil and then add the white gravy,

spinach purée, black salt and salt. Stir for about 1 minute.
5. Add the *paneer* cubes, dried fenugreek leaves, Punjabi *garam masala*, sugar and cream and bring to a boil.
    Serve hot.

Variation : MUTTER PALAK

Use 2 cups of boiled green peas instead of the *paneer* cubes.

MUSHROOM PALAK

Use 2 cups sautéed mushrooms instead of the paneer cubes.

❧ Makhani Paneer ❧

This lip smacking preparation is popular in almost all Indian states... originally of North Indian origin, every state adds a distinct touch to this recipe. Already laden with butter, this gravy tastes even richer when served topped with a dollop of butter.

Preparation time: 15 minutes.   Cooking time: 45 minutes.   Serves 4.

2½ cups *paneer* (cottage cheese), cut into cubes
1 bayleaf *(tejpatta)*
25 mm. (1") piece cinnamon *(dalichin)*
2 cloves *(laung / lavang)*
2 cardamoms *(elaichi)*
2 tsp ginger-garlic paste
½ cup fresh thick curds *(dahi)*, whisked
3 tbsp tomato ketchup
1 tsp Punjabi *garam masala*, page 100
2 tsp dried fenugreek leaves *(kasuri methi)*
½ tsp sugar
2 tbsp cream

2 tbsp butter
Salt to taste

For the makhani gravy
1 cup chopped tomatoes
½ cup sliced onions
¼ cup cashewnuts *(kaju)*
2 whole dry red chillies

For the garnish
1 tsp butter

For the makhani curry
1. Combine all the ingredients with 1½ cups of water and simmer for about 30 minutes.
2. Cool and blend into a smooth paste. Keep aside.

How to proceed
1. Heat the butter in a pan and add the bayleaf, cinnamon, cloves and cardamom to it.
2. Add the ginger-garlic paste and sauté for a few seconds.
3. Add the makhani gravy, curds, tomato ketchup and salt and simmer for about 5 minutes.
4. Add about ¼ cup of water if required to adjust the consistency of the gravy.
5. Add the paneer, Punjabi *garam masala*, dried fenugreek leaves, sugar and cream and simmer for 3 to 4 minutes.
   Serve hot garnished with butter.

❦ Paneer Tava Masala ❦

Picture on back cover.

Try the Punjabi version of this ever popular dish. Carefully combined spices ranging from ajwain to shah jeera, make this a real culinary treat!

Preparation time: 15 minutes.   Cooking time: 20 minutes.   Serves 4.

3 cups *paneer* (cottage cheese), cut into 1" x ½" cubes
2 tbsp dried fenugreek leaves *(kasuri methi)*, crushed
1 tsp chilli powder
½ tsp turmeric powder *(haldi)*
1 tsp chaat masala
½ tsp *ajwain* (carom seeds)
½ tsp cumin seeds *(jeera)*
½ cup chopped onions
2 tsp garlic paste
1 tsp chopped green chillies
1 tsp coriander *(dhania)* powder
½ cup fresh tomato purée, page 102

¼ tsp caraway seeds *(shah jeera)*, roasted
2 tbsp fresh cream
½ tsp Punjabi *garam masala*, page 100
6 tbsp oil
Salt to taste

For the garnish
2 tbsp chopped coriander

1. Marinate the *paneer* cubes with dried fenugreek leaves, chilli powder, turmeric powder, chaat masala and salt. Keep aside for ½ hour.
2. Heat 3 tbsp of oil in a non-stick pan and shallow-fry the *paneer* pieces in it till they are golden brown in colour.
3. Drain on absorbent paper and keep aside.
4. Heat the remaining oil on a tava and add the *ajwain* and cumin seeds to it.
5. When they crackle, add the onions and sauté till they turn translucent.
6. Add the garlic paste, green chillies, coriander powder and salt and sauté for 2 minutes.
7. Add the tomato purée and caraway seeds. Cook till the oil separates from the gravy.
8. Add the fried *paneer* cubes, cream and Punjabi *garam masala* and mix gently. Serve hot garnished with coriander.

❧ Kadhai Paneer ❧

A tantalizing dish to rustle up when you are in a hurry. Replace the paneer with mixed boiled vegetables to make subz kadhai.

Preparation time: 15 minutes.   Cooking time: 25 minutes.   Serves 4.

3 cups *paneer* (cottage cheese), cut into 1" cubes
1 tsp coriander *(dhania)* seeds, dry roasted and crushed
1 tsp ginger-garlic paste
1½ cups chopped tomatoes
1 tsp chilli powder
¼ cup cream
1 tsp dried fenugreek leaves *(kasuri methi)*
¼ tsp cardamom *(elaichi)* powder
¼ tsp Punjabi *garam masala,* page 100
2 tbsp butter
Salt to taste

Other ingredients
Oil for deep-frying

For the garnish
2 tbsp chopped coriander

1. Deep-fry the *paneer* cubes till they are golden brown.
2. Drain on absorbent paper and then put them in warm water for 15 minutes.
3. Drain again and keep aside.
4. Heat the butter in a *kadhai*, add the coriander and sauté for half a minute.
5. Add the ginger-garlic paste and sauté for another minute.
6. Add the tomatoes and sauté till the oil separates from the gravy.
7. Add the chilli powder, cream and dried fenugreek leaves and salt and simmer for some time.
8. Add the *paneer*, cardamom and Punjabi *garam masala* and heat for a few more minutes.
   Serve hot garnished with coriander.

❧ Pasanda Paneer ❧

Soft tikkis and spicy gravy are made for each other! In case you are in a hurry you can avoid making tikkis and just use paneer cubes instead.

Preparation time: 25 minutes.   Cooking time: 25 minutes.   Serves 4.

For the tikkis
1½ cups grated *paneer* (cottage cheese)
1 tsp chopped green chillies
¼ tsp freshly ground peppercorns
2 tbsp plain flour *(maida)*
Bread crumbs for coating
2 tbsp oil
Salt to taste

For paste no.1
¾ cup chopped onions
5 cloves garlic
12mm. (½") piece ginger

2 tbsp cashewnuts *(kaju)*

For paste no.2
½ cup sliced onions
Oil for deep-frying

For the gravy
¾ cup fresh thick curds *(dahi)*, whisked
1 tsp chilli powder
½ tsp Punjabi *garam masala*, page 100
2 tbsp oil or ghee
Salt to taste

For the garnish
2 tbsp chopped coriander

For the tikkis
1. Combine all the ingredients except the bread crumbs and oil and mix well.
2. Shape into flat round tikkis and roll in bread crumbs.
3. Heat the oil on a non-stick *tava* and cook on both sides till they are golden brown.

For paste no. 1
1. Combine all the ingredients with 1 cup of water and boil for 15-20 minutes.
2. Cool and blend in a mixer to a smooth paste. Keep aside.

For paste no. 2
1. Deep-fry the onions in oil until golden brown.
2. Drain on absorbent paper and blend to a smooth paste in a blender. Keep aside.

For the gravy
1. Heat the oil in a pan, add the paste no. 1 and cook on a low flame for a few minutes.
2. Add the chilli powder and Punjabi *garam masala*, mix well and cook again for a few minutes.

3. Add the curds, mix well and cook for 5 minutes while stirring continuously.
4. Add the paste no.2, salt and cook till oil separates from the gravy.
5. Add ½ cup of water and bring to a boil.

How to proceed
Arrange the *paneer tikkis* in a plate. Pour the hot gravy on the top.
Serve hot garnished with coriander.

❖ Paneer and Baby Corn Jalfrazie ❖

Picture on page 55.

An absolute fusion taste… jalfrazie charged with Punjabi garam masala!

Preparation time: 10 minutes.   Cooking time: 15 minutes.   Serves 4.

1½ cups *paneer* (cottage cheese), cut into 1" cubes
1 cup baby corn, cut into 4 lengthwise
3 tbsp sliced onions
¾ cup capsicum, cut into strips
¼ tsp turmeric powder *(haldi)*
½ tsp chilli powder
½ tsp coriander-cumin seed *(dhania-jeera)* powder
½ cup tomato, cut into strips
2 tbsp tomato ketchup
2 tbsp fresh tomato purée, page 102
2 tsp vinegar
½ tsp Punjabi *garam masala*, page 100
¼ tsp sugar
1 tbsp oil

53

Salt to taste

For the garnish
2 tbsp chopped coriander

1. Heat the oil in a pan and add the onions and capsicum and sauté for 2 minutes.
2. Add the baby corn, turmeric powder, chilli powder, coriander-cumin seed powder, tomatoes, tomato ketchup, tomato purée and salt and sauté on a slow flame for 4 to 5 minutes till the baby corn is cooked.
3. Add the *paneer*, vinegar, Punjabi *garam masala* and sugar and toss lightly. Garnish with coriander and serve hot.

❖ Paneer Kalimirch ❖

A rich preparation of paneer coated slightly with a fiery gravy charged with freshly crushed pepper.

Preparation time: 10 minutes.   Cooking time: 25 minutes.   Serves 4.

2 cups *paneer* (cottage cheese), cut into ½" cubes
¼ cup fresh cream
½ cup milk
¼ tsp Punjabi *garam masala*, page 100
1 tsp freshly crushed peppercorns
2 tbsp oil
Salt to taste

To be ground into a smooth paste
1½ cups chopped onions
½ cup broken cashewnuts *(kaju)*
4 cloves garlic

6 mm. (¼") piece ginger
2 tbsp water

For the garnish
1 tbsp chopped coriander
1 tbsp chopped mint leaves (*phudina*)

1. Heat the oil in a pan and fry the paste for 4 to 5 minutes while stirring continuously.
2. Add the *paneer*, cream, milk, salt and 1 cup of water and bring to a boil.
3. Add the Punjabi *garam masala* and crushed peppercorns and mix well. Serve hot garnished with coriander and mint.

Jaade Ki Subzi

Sarson Ka Saag

Picture on cover.

This traditional dish has no variations due to its extreme simplicity. This dish is made every alternate day in winter in all Punjabi households. For the real experience, this should be enjoyed with makkai ki roti and Punjabi lassi!

Preparation time: 15 minutes.   Cooking time: 30 minutes.   Serves 4.

5 cups *sarson ka saag* (mustard leaves)
1½ cups spinach *(palak)* or ½ cup bhatua bhaji
¼ cup chopped onions
3 tsp chopped green chillies
2 tsp chopped ginger
3 tbsp maize flour *(makkai ka atta)*
¼ cup milk
½ cup fresh tomato purée, page 102
2 tsp chilli powder

2 tbsp ghee
Salt to taste

For serving
Makkai ki roti, page 93

1. Cook *sarson ka saag*, spinach, green chillies and ginger with 1½ cups of water for 15 to 20 minutes.
2. Once cooked blend to a coarse paste in a blender.
3. Dissolve the maize flour with milk and add it to the blended paste.
4. Cook for 3 to 4 minutes on a low flame. Keep aside.
5. Heat the ghee in another pan and add the onions.
6. Sauté till they turn translucent and then add the tomato purée.
7. Cook stirring continuously till the mixture leaves oil.
8. Add the chilli powder and the prepared paste and simmer for 5 to 6 minutes. Serve hot with makkai ki roti.

❀ Shalgam ki Subzi ❀

Shalgam or turnip, a member of the radish family that tastes much milder, is a winter vegetable that is strongly associated with Punjabi cuisine. In fact, no other cuisine makes such extensive use of the vegetable. Turnips cook easily, and taste fantastic when combined with tomatoes as in this semi-dry curry.

Preparation time: 20 minutes.   Cooking time: 25 minutes.   Serves 4.

3 cups peeled turnips (*shalgam*), cut into ¼" thick slices
1 tsp cumin seeds (*jeera*)
1 tsp ginger-garlic paste
¼ tsp turmeric powder (*haldi*)
1 tsp cumin seed (*jeera*) powder
1 tsp red chilli powder
½ cup chopped tomatoes
½ tsp Punjabi *garam masala*, page 100
2 tbsp chopped coriander
4 tbsp oil
Salt to taste

1. Heat the oil in a pan and add cumin seeds.
2. When they crackle add in ginger-garlic paste, turmeric powder, cumin powder, chilli powder, salt and turnips.
3. Sauté the turnips in the masala for 2 minutes. Add ¼ cup of water cover and cook till the turnips are soft.
4. Remove the lid and add tomatoes, Punjabi *garam masala* and coriander. Cook for 5 minutes.
   Serve hot.

Handy tip : If you want to use larger pieces of turnip, parboil them in salted water before adding them to the *subzi*

❖ Kamal Kakdi ki Subzi ❖

Lotus stems taste very similar to water cress (singoda), and acquire an exotic flavour in this innovative gravy which combines tomatoes and brinjals. The roundels look like pretty small wheels, adding visual appeal also to this tasty dish!

Preparation time: 15 minutes.   Cooking time: 15 minutes.   Serves 4.

½ kg lotus stem (*kamal kakdi / bhein*)
1 cup peeled and chopped brinjals (*baingan*)
1 cup chopped tomatoes
2 cloves (*laung / lavang*)
25 mm. (1") stick cinnamon (*dalchini*)
2 bayleaves (tejpatta)
¼ tsp turmeric powder (*haldi*)
1½ tsp coriander-cumin seed (*dhania- jeera*) powder
2 tsps chilli powder
1 tsp dry mango powder (*amchur*)
4 tbsp oil
Salt to taste

To be ground into an onion paste
1 cup chopped onions
1 tsp chopped ginger
4 small cloves of garlic

For the garnish
2 tbsp chopped coriander

1. Wash the lotus stem well. Peel and slice into ¼" thick roundels and parboil in 4 cups of water with turmeric and salt.
2. Drain and keep aside.
3. Heat 1 tbsp of oil in a pan and cook the brinjal pieces in it on a slow flame until soft.
4. Blend the brinjal pieces and tomato pulp in a blender to a smooth paste. Keep aside.
5. Heat the remaining 3 tbsp of oil and sauté the cloves, cinnamon and bayleaves in it for 1 minute. Add the onion paste and sauté till it turns translucent.
6. Add the tomato-brinjal paste, turmeric powder, coriander-cumin seed powder, chilli powder and salt. Cook till the oil separates from the gravy.
7. Add the cooked lotus stem, dry mango powder and ¾ cup water and simmer for a few minutes.
   Serve hot garnished with coriander.

❖ Crispy Arbi Subzi ❖

Picture on facing page.

This dry dish of crispy rice-coated arbi pieces goes extremely well with moist dal and parathas.

Preparation time: 15 minutes.   Cooking time: 25 minutes.   Serves 4.

½ kg colocasia (*arbi*)
1 cup beaten rice (*poha*)
3 whole dry red chillies, dry roasted and broken into pieces
¼ tsp asafoetida (*hing*)
1 tsp turmeric powder (*haldi*)
1 tsp mustard seeds (*rai / sarson*)
2 tbsp oil
Salt to taste

CRISYPY ARBI SUBZI : Recipe above. ↪

1. Wash the colocasia thoroughly. Pressure cook in a vessel over water for 2 whistles. Make sure the colocasia is cooked but not overcooked.
2. Remove and peel the colocasia. Cut into ¼" thick roundels. Keep aside.
3. Grind together the beaten rice, red chillies, asafoetida and turmeric powder to a fine powder. Keep aside.
4. Heat the oil in a pan and add the cumin seeds in it.
5. When they crackle, add the colocasia, salt and the ground powder. Stir-fry till the mixture is crisp.

Serve hot.

❖ Arbi Naveli ❖

Deep fried arbi in an exotic gravy. The spices vie with one another to add more exquisiteness to the dish!

Preparation time: 15 minutes.   Cooking time: 20 minutes.   Serves 4.

250 gms colocasia (*arbi*)
1½ tbsp *besan* (Bengal gram flour)
1 tsp chilli powder
½ tsp Punjabi *garam masala*, page 100
½ cup fresh tomato purée, page 102
½ tsp dry mango powder (*amchur*)
2 tbsp whisked curds (*dahi*)
½ cup milk
2 tbsp oil
Salt to taste

For the paste
1 tbsp poppy seeds (*khus-khus*)
1 tbsp melon seeds
2 medium sized onions
3 to 4 flakes garlic
25mm. (1") piece ginger

Other ingredients
Oil for deep-frying

For the paste
1. Soak the poppy seeds and melon seeds in ½ cup of warm water for 15 minutes. Keep aside.
2. Grind together the onion, garlic, ginger and soaked seeds to a very fine paste.

How to proceed
1. Pressure-cook the colocasia in a vessel over water for 2 whistles.
2. Peel and slice them into ¼" thick round slices.
3. Mix together the salt, ½ tsp chilli powder and *besan*. Lightly coat the colocasia slices with the mixture.
4. Heat enough oil in a *kadhai* and deep-fry the colocasia till golden brown and crisp. Drain on absorbent paper and keep aside.
5. Heat the oil in a pan and sauté the ground paste till brown.
6. Add the tomato purée, Punjabi *garam masala*, dry mango powder, remaining ½ tsp chilli powder and salt. Cook till the oil separates from the gravy.
7. Add in the curds and milk. Simmer the gravy for 2 to 3 minutes.
8. Add the colocasia and mix well.
   Serve hot.

❖ Aloo Mutter Korma ❖

Who said Punjabi kormas are non-vegetarian? This Aloo Mutter Korma stands testimony to the fact that vegetables can do justice to the korma recipe too!

Preparation time: 15 minutes.   Cooking time: 30 minutes.   Serves 4.

15 small potatoes, boiled and peeled
1½ cups boiled green peas
2 tbsp fresh thick curds (*dahi*), whisked
¼ cup cream
½ tsp Punjabi *garam masala*, page 100
1 tsp butter
2 tbsp ghee
Salt to taste

For the paste

1 cup roughly chopped onions
2 tbsp broken cashewnuts (*kaju*)
1 tsp chopped ginger
1 tsp chopped green chillies

For the paste

1. Combine all the ingredients for the paste with 1 cup of water and cook for 15-20 minutes.
2. Blend to a smooth paste in a blender and keep aside.

How to proceed

1. Heat the ghee in a pan, add the prepared paste and sauté till the mixture leaves oil.
2. Add the potatoes, peas, curds, cream and salt and simmer for 3-4 minutes.
3. Add the Punjabi *garam masala* and butter and mix well.
   Serve hot.

Variation : ZAFFRANI PANEER KORMA

Just add 2 cups of fried *paneer* (cottage cheese) cubes and ¼ tsp of roasted saffron (*kesar*) to the recipe at step 2 instead of potatoes and peas.

❧ Dhingri Mutter ❧

This rare combination of mushrooms and peas in tomato gravy goes to show that mushrooms, though seen as International ingredient, are very popular in North India too.

Preparation time: 15 minutes.   Cooking time: 30 minutes.   Serves 4.

2 cups mushrooms (*dhingri*), cut into quarters
1 cup boiled green peas
2 tbsp tomato ketchup
1 tsp chilli powder
A pinch of Punjabi *garam masala*, page 100
¼ cup chopped coriander
2 tbsp cream
1 tbsp butter
Salt to taste

½ cup chopped tomatoes
1½ tbsp melon seeds
1 green chilli
2 whole dry Kashmiri red chillies
6 mm. (¼") piece ginger
1 tsp chopped garlic
5 tsp oil

For the gravy
1 cup sliced onions

For the gravy

1. Heat 3 tsp of oil in a pan, add the onions and sauté them till the turn golden brown. Keep aside.
2. Combine the tomatoes, melon seeds, green chilli, red chillies, ginger and garlic with ½ cup of water and simmer on a low flame for 10 to 15 minutes. Cool and keep aside.
3. Blend to a smooth paste along with the browned onions.
4. Heat the remaining 2 tsp of oil and sauté this paste for 15 to 20 minutes till the mixture leaves oil.

How to proceed

1. Heat the butter in a pan, add the mushrooms and peas and sauté till the mushrooms and peas and sauté till the mushrooms are almost done.
2. Add the prepared gravy, tomato ketchup, chilli powder, Punjabi *garam masala*, coriander, cream, salt and ½ cup water and mix well.
3. Simmer for 2 to 3 minutes while stirring continuously.
   Serve hot.

Khoya Mutter Makhana

Picture on page 75.

Exotic makhanas in a sinfully rich khoya based gravy.

Preparation time: 10 minutes.   Cooking time: 25 minutes.   Serves 6.

¾ cup khoya *(mava)*
2 cups green peas
1 cup lotus seeds *(makhana)*
2 tsp cumin *(jeera)* powder
2 tsp Punjabi *garam masala,* page 100
1 tsp turmeric powder *(haldi)*
1 tsp chilli powder
2 big tomatoes, blanched and chopped
2 tbsp broken cashewnuts *(kaju)*
4 tbsp oil
Salt to taste

To be ground into a paste
2 medium sized onions
25 mm. (1") piece ginger

For the garnish
2 tbsp chopped coriander

1. Heat 2 tbsp of oil in a pan and sauté the lotus seeds in it till they are golden brown. Remove and keep aside.
2. Put the khoya in the same oil and fry till the mixture leaves the sides of the pan. Remove and keep aside.
3. Heat the remaining oil in the pan, add the ground paste, cumin powder, Punjabi *garam masala*, turmeric powder, chilli powder and salt. Mix well.
4. Add the tomatoes and cook till the mixture leaves oil.
5. Add the peas and 2½ cups of water and cook till the peas are almost tender.
6. Add the lotus seeds and cook till lotus seeds and peas are cooked.
7. Add the khoya and cashewnuts and fry for 2 minutes.
   Serve hot garnished with coriander.

KHOYA MUTTER MAKHANA : Recipe on page 73. ➜

❦ Chana Palak ❦

A rare combination of palak and chana in an even more exotic gravy of brinjals and tomatoes!

Preparation time: 20 minutes.   Cooking time: 25 minutes.   Serves 6.

1 cup kabuli chana *(chick peas)*
5 medium sized brinjals *(baingan)*
1 cup chopped tomatoes
1 tsp cumin seeds *(jeera)*
25 mm. (1") stick cinnamon *(dalchini)*
2 cloves *(laung / lavang)*
2 bayleaves *(tejpatta)*
1 tsp Punjabi *garam masala,* page 100
2 tsp chilli powder
1 tsp dry mango powder *(amchur)*
1 tsp coriander-cumin seed *(dhania-jeera)* powder
1½ cups chopped spinach *(palak)*

A pinch soda bi-carb
6 tbsp oil
Salt to taste

To be ground into a paste
 3 medium sized onions, roughly chopped
8 cloves garlic
25 mm. (1") piece ginger

1. Soak the *kabuli chana* overnight. Next day, boil in a pressure cooker with a little water and the soda bi-carb. Drain and keep aside..
2. Skin the brinjals and cut into small pieces. Heat 1 tbsp of oil and cook the brinjal pieces on a slow flame until soft.
3. Blend the brinjal and tomato in a mixer to a smooth paste and keep aside.
4. Heat the oil in a pan, add the cumin seeds. When they crackle, add the tomato-brinjal paste, Punjabi *garam masala* and chilli powder and fry for 5 minutes.
5. Add the *kabuli chana,* dry mango powder, coriander-cumin seed powder and salt and cook for a few minutes.
6. Add the spinach and cook for 3 minutes.
    Serve hot.

❧ Methi Mutter Malai ❧

This popular Punjabi dish is made with fresh fenugreek leaves and green peas.

Preparation time: 20 minutes.   Cooking time: 15 minutes.   Serves 6.

2½ cups chopped fenugreek (methi) leaves
½ tsp cumin seeds *(jeera)*
½ cup chopped onions
¾ cup fresh tomato purée, page 102
1 cup boiled green peas
1 cup milk
A pinch of sugar
3 tbsp oil
Salt to taste

To be ground into a paste
1 onion, roughly chopped
3 green chillies
25 mm. (1") piece ginger
3 cloves garlic
2 tbsp cashewnuts
2 tsp *khus-khus* (poppy seeds)

For the dry masala (to be roasted lightly and powdered)
2 small sticks cinnamon *(dalchini)*
4 cloves *(laung / lavang)*
2 cardamoms *(elaichi)*
4 peppercorns
1 tsp cumin seeds *(jeera)*

1. Wash the fenugreek leaves. Add ½ tsp of salt. Keep aside for 15 minutes and then squeeze out the water.
2. Heat 2 tbsp of oil in a pan, add the cumin seeds when they crackle, add the fenugreek leaves and cook for 3 to 4 minutes. Remove and keep aside.
3. Add the remaining 1 tbsp of oil in the same pan and heat again. Add the onions and sauté till they are golden brown.

4. Add the paste and sauté for 1 minute. Add the tomato purée and dry masala and sauté again till the mixture leaves oil.
5. Add the peas, fenugreek leaves, milk, sugar, salt and a little water and cook for a few minutes.
   Serve hot.

Bharvan Simla Mirch

Bharvan is a typical North Indian preparation, which can be prepared with different vegetables like karelas, tindas etc. It is the stuffing that is the unique aspect of bharvan. Some bharvan dishes are with gravies, while some like this can just be served as a dry snack.

Preparation time: 10 minutes.   Cooking time: 15 minutes.   Serves 6.

4 big capsicum
4 tbsp *besan* (Bengal gram flour)
1 tsp chilli powder
4 tbsp oil
Salt to taste

2 tsp dry mango powder (*amchur*)
1 tsp coriander-cumin seed (*dhania-jeera*) powder
1 tbsp Punjabi *garam masala,* page 100
2 tbsp oil
Salt to taste

For the stuffing
2 cups boiled and mashed potatoes
½ cup chopped capsicum
1 tsp cumin seeds (*jeera*)
1 tsp turmeric powder (*haldi*)
1 tsp chilli powder

For the gravy
5 big tomatoes, cut into big pieces
3 tbsp cashewnuts
½ tsp cumin seeds (*jeera*)
12 mm. (½") stick cinnamon (*dalchini*)
2 cloves (*laung / lavang*)

1 tsp chilli powder
2 tsp sugar
¼ cup cream
2 tbsp oil
Salt to taste

For the stuffing
1. Heat the oil in a pan and add the cumin seeds.
2. When the seeds crackle, add the capsicum and sauté for a minute.
3. Add all the remaining ingredients and cook till the mixture becomes dry.

How to proceed
1. Cut the stem of the capsicum and de-seed them. Cut into half vertically.
2. Stuff the hollow capsicums with the prepared stuffing. Keep aside.
3. Make a paste of the *besan,* chilli powder and salt with 4 tbsp of water. Keep aside.
4. Heat the oil in a non-stick pan, coat the filling side of the capsicum with the prepared paste and cook them in hot oil (filling side down) on a low flame till the coating is golden brown.
5. Turn the capsicum and cook the other side for ½ a minute.
6. Remove and keep aside.

For the gravy
1. Combine the tomatoes and cashewnuts with 1 cup of water and cook till for about 20 minutes on a medium flame.
2. When cooked blend in a blender to a smooth paste.
3. Strain and keep aside.
4. Heat the oil in a pan, add the cumin seeds, cinnamon and cloves.
5. When the cumin seeds crackle, add the tomato purée, chilli powder, sugar and salt and simmer for 4-5 minutes.
6. Add the cream and simmer for 3-4 minutes. Keep aside.

How to proceed
Arrange the stuffed capsicum in a serving dish. Pour the hot gravy on top.
Serve hot.

✤ Malai Kofta ✤

Picture on facing page.

With Malai Kofta, it is always celebration time! This is one dish which nobody will get bored of even if it is served at every party. The koftas themselves are so tasty that they can easily be served as a snack along with tea.

Preparation time: 30 minutes.   Cooking time: 40 minutes.   Serves 6.

For the koftas
½ cup grated *paneer* (cottage cheese)
½ cup boiled and grated potatoes
1 tbsp milk powder
1 tbsp tomato ketchup
1 tsp chilli powder
A pinch turmeric powder (*haldi*)
¼ cup grated carrots
2 tbsp finely chopped capsicum
1 tsp grated ginger
½ tsp grated garlic
1 tbsp chopped coriander

MALAI KOFTA : Recipe above. ➜

Oil for deep frying
Salt to taste

For the gravy
1½ cups fresh tomato purée, page 102
2 large onions, roughly chopped
2 cloves *(laung / lavang)*
2 small sticks cinnamon *(dalchini)*
1 tbsp cashewnut *(kaju)* paste
1 tsp sugar
1 tsp Punjabi *garam masala*, page 100
1 tsp chilli powder
2 tbsp cream
4 tbsp butter
salt to taste

To be ground into a paste (for the gravy)
15 cloves garlic
25 mm. (1") piece ginger
5 green chillies

For the garnish
1 tbsp chopped coriander

For the koftas
1. Combine all the ingredients together and divide it into 8 equal portions.
2. Roll each portion into a cylindrical shape and deep-fry them over a medium flame in hot oil till they are golden brown. Drain on absorbent paper and keep aside.

For the gravy
1. Blend the onions in a mixer with very little water to a smooth paste. Keep aside.
2. Heat the butter in a pan, add the prepared paste, onion paste and stir-fry for 5 minutes till the mixture is golden brown.
3. Add the cloves, cinnamon and cashew paste and fry again for 2 minutes.
4. Add the tomato purée and cook till the mixture leaves oil.
5. Add 1 cup of water and bring to a boil.
6. Add the Punjabi *garam masala*, chilli powder, cream and salt and simmer for 5 minutes.

How to proceed
Arrange the *koftas* in a serving dish. Pour the gravy over the *koftas*. Garnish with coriander.
Serve hot.

❖ Subz Bahar ❖

An assortment of vegetables in luxurious white gravy an unbeatable recipe from the Punjabi khazana!

Preparation time: 30 minutes.   Cooking time: 20 minutes.   Serves 4.

1 cup *paneer* (cottage cheese) cubes
2 cups mixed boiled vegetables (carrots, french beans, cauliflower, green peas)
2 tbsp poppy seeds *(khus-khus)*
1 tbsp broken cashewnuts *(kaju)*
¼ cup milk
2 bayleaves *(tejpatta)*
4 cloves *(laung / lavang)*
1 tsp Punjabi *garam masala,* page 100
3 tbsp fresh cream
2 tbsp oil
Salt to taste

To be ground to a onion paste
1 onion, chopped roughly
3 green chillies
12 mm. (½") piece ginger
3 cloves garlic

1. Soak the poppy seeds and cashewnuts in milk for ½ hour. Grind to a smooth paste in a blender and keep aside.
2. Heat the oil in a pan, add the bayleaves and cloves and sauté for a minute. Add the onion paste and sauté till the mixture turns golden brown.
3. Add the poppy seeds-cashewnut paste and salt and sauté again till the oil separates from the gravy.
4. Add the *paneer*, vegetables, Punjabi *garam masala* and cream, mix well and simmer for 3 to 4 minutes.
   Serve hot.

❧ Bharvan Baingan ❧

A tangy paste plays a dual role in this dish as a filling and as a base for the gravy. Remember to cook the brinjals on a slow flame to enable them to impart a better taste to the dish.

Preparation time: 20 minutes.   Cooking time: 30 minutes.   Serves 4.

10 to 12 small brinjals
½ tsp cumin seeds (*jeera*)
½ cup chopped onions
¼ cup chopped coriander
3 tbsp oil
Salt to taste

For the paste
½ tsp fenugreek (*methi*) seeds
1 large cardamom (*elaichi*)
2 bayleaves (*tejpatta*)
25mm. (1") stick cinnamon (*dalchini*)

¼ cup coriander *(dhania)* seeds
1 tsp cumin seeds *(jeera)*
1 tsp grated ginger
¾ cup chopped onions
½ tsp turmeric powder *(haldi)*
5 whole dry red chillies, soaked in warm water
½ tsp dry mango powder *(amchur)*
½ cup chopped tomatoes
2 tbsp oil
Salt to taste

For the paste
1. Heat the oil in a pan and sauté the fenugreek seeds, cardamom, bayleaves, cinnamon, coriander seeds, cumin seeds and ginger over a slow flame till they are lightly browned. Cool completely.
2. Grind all the ingredients for the paste using ¼ cup of water in a blender till smooth. Keep aside.

How to proceed
1. Slit the brinjals in the centre to make a criss-cross mark that divides each brinjal into 4 parts joined at the stem.

2. Fill the slits with the ground paste, keeping some aside to use later.
3. Heat the oil in a pan and add the cumin seeds.
4. When they crackle, add the onions and sauté till they are golden brown.
5. Add the stuffed brinjals and top with the remaining paste.
6. Cover and cook over a slow flame till the brinjals are soft. Add about ¼ cup of water if required.
7. Add the coriander and mix well.
   Serve hot.

Subzi Ke Saath

❧ Makkai ki Roti ❧

Delicious rotis made from healthy makkai ka atta.

Preparation time: 30 minutes.   Cooking time: 15 minutes.   Makes 5 roti.

2 cups maize flour *(makai ka atta)*
¼ tsp salt

Other ingredients
Hot water for kneading
2 tsp butter to serve

1. Combine all the ingredients and knead into firm dough using enough hot water. Allow it to rest for 30 minutes, under a damp muslin cloth.
2. Divide the dough into 5 equal portions and roll out each portion to make a flat circle of about 125 mm. (5") in diameter.
3. Half cook on a *tava* (griddle) on both sides and when serving cook directly on flame.
   Serve hot with butter.

❖ Lachha Parathas ❖

Making this flaky, layered paratha is an art by itself. As soon as these parathas are cooked, they are pressed from all sides to separate out the layers.

Preparation time: 20 minutes.   Cooking time: 20 minutes.   Makes 8 parathas.

3 cups plain flour *(maida)*
3 tbsp oil
1 tsp salt

Other ingredients
Warm water for kneading
Oil for rolling and cooking
Butter for serving

1. Sieve the flour and salt together in bowl. Rub in the oil and add enough warm water gradually. Knead to smooth dough. Cover with a wet muslin cloth and leave aside for 20 minutes.

2. Knead again and divide the dough into 8 portions. Shape individually into even-sized rounds.
3. Roll out each dough round into a circle of 150 mm. (6") diameter. Cut into 50 mm. (2") strips lengthways. Place all the strips over the center one.
4. Roll up like a Swiss roll. Press a little with your fingers. Pour ½ tsp of oil on each roll.
5. Take one roll at a time and roll it out into a circle of about 125 mm. (5") diameter.
6. Place it on your palms and lightly press towards the centre to show the layers clearly.
7. Heat a *tava* (griddle) and cook the rounds lightly on both sides. When you want to serve, cook the rounds directly on the gas or preferably on charcoal.
   Apply butter and serve hot.

❖ Aam ka Achaar ❖

The combination of fennel and nigella seeds with mustard and other pickling spices is what distinguishes this mango pickle from its Gujarati counterpart methia keri. This is a very simple recipe to follow. Just keep in mind the basics of pickle making use a clean sterilised jar, see that there is no moisture, and ensure that mustard oil forms a protective layer over the ingredients in the jar.

Preparation time: 4 hours.   Cooking time: Nil.   Makes 2 cups.
Maturing Time: 4 to 5 days.   Storage upto 1 year: In a cool dry place.

3 cups (375 gms) raw mangoes, cut into 25 mm. (1") pieces
1 tsp turmeric powder *(haldi)*
¼ cup fennel seeds *(saunf)*, coarsely ground
1 tbsp crushed fenugreek seeds *(methi na kuria)*
2 tbsp split mustard seeds *(rai na kuria)*
½ tsp nigella seeds *(kalonji)*
¼ tsp asafoetida *(hing)*
2 tbsp chilli powder
½ cup mustard oil
4 tbsp salt

1. Combine the mangoes, turmeric powder and 2 tbsp of salt and toss well.
2. Place the mangoes on a sieve, cover with a clean muslin cloth and place under the sun for 4 to 6 hours.
3. Combine the rest of the ingredients in a bowl and mix well.
4. Add the mangoes and toss well.
5. Bottle the pickle in a sterilised glass jar. Place the pickle under the sun for 4 to 5 days. This pickle can be stored for upto 1 year in a cool dry place.

❖ Palak ka Raita ❖

Palak is indeed an all-time favourite up north. It comes as a surprise that palak tastes extremely good as a raita too!

Preparation time: 5 minutes.   Cooking time: 1 minutes.   Serves 4.

2 cups spinach (*palak*) leaves, shredded
2 cups fresh thick curds (*dahi*)
1 tsp roasted and crushed cumin seeds (*jeera*)
½ tsp black salt (*sanchal*)
Salt to taste

Other ingredients
Oil for deep-frying

1. Put a few spinach leaves in a metal strainer and deep-fry by dipping the spinach-filled strainer in hot oil for half a minute. Repeat for all the remaining spinach leaves.
2. Drain on absorbent paper and keep aside.

3. Combine all the remaining ingredients and whisk well.
4. Add the spinach and mix well.
   Serve immediately.

Basic Recipe

❖ Punjabi Garam Masala ❖

This is a must-have item, which you ought to prepare and store before trying your hand at Punjabi cooking! You can store Punjabi garam masala in an air-tight container for upto a year but if you do not have the time or inclination to make it, use any garam masala available in the market.

Preparation time: 15 minutes.   Cooking time: 2 minutes.   Makes 2 cups.

100 gms cumin seeds (*jeera*)
75 gms cardamom seeds (*elaichi*)
65 gms peppercorn
35 gms coriander (*dhania*) seeds
35 gms fennel seeds (*saunf*)
20 gms cloves (*laung / lavang*)
15 gms cinnamon (*dalchini*)
20 gms mace (*javantri*), optional

20 gms caraway seeds (*shahjeera*)
15 gms bayleaves (*tejpatta*)
15 gms ginger powder (*soonth*)
3 nutmeg (*jaiphal*)

1. Dry roast all the ingredients except the ginger powder on a *tava* (griddle) till you get an aroma of the spices.
2. Grind them to a fine powder in a grinder.
3. Add the ginger powder and mix well.
4. Sieve and store in an air-tight container.
   Use as required.

❖ Fresh Tomato Purée ❖

While it is tempting to pick a pack of tomato purée off the store shelf, home-made purée is always more tasty and sans the preservatives. The recipes in this book are all based on the following home-made purée recipe, and using commercially available purée may require you to tweak the recipes a little according to the purée concentration. Fresh tomato purée can be made at home in a jiffy. To store it, just pour it into ice cube trays, freeze, pop out, and store in the freezer in an airtight plastic freezer box or Ziploc bag. This will stay nice and fresh for upto two months, waiting to be added to your yummy gravies!

Preparation time: 5 minutes.   Cooking time: 2 minutes.   Makes approx. ¾ cups.

2 medium sized tomatoes

1. Bring to a boil a large vessel full of water.
2. Scoop out and discard the eyes of the tomatoes using the tip of the sharp knife.
3. Make criss-cross cuts at the base of each tomato.
4. Put in boiling water for 3 to 4 minutes.
5. Remove and put in cold water for some time.
6. When the tomatoes are cool, peel and discard the skin.
7. Chop roughly and blend to a smooth purée in a blender. Use as required.